To: _____

From: _____

Other books by Gregory E. Lang:

Why a Daughter Needs a Dad

Why a Daughter Needs a Mom

Why a Son Needs a Dad

Why I Love Grandma

Why I Love Grandpa

Why I Chose You

Why I Love You

Why I Still Love You

Why I Need You

Why We Are a Family

Why We Are Friends

Brothers and Sisters

Simple Acts

Love Signs

Life Maps

Thank You, Mom

Thank You, Dad

Why a Son Needs a Mom

· 100 Reasons ·

GREGORY E. LANG

CUMBERLAND HOUSE

NASHVILLE, TENNESSEE

WHY A SON NEEDS A MOM
Published by Cumberland House Publishing, Inc.
431 Harding Industrial Drive
Nashville, TN 37211

Copyright © 2004 by Gregory E. Lang

ISBN-13: 978-1-58182-655-5
ISBN-10: 1-58182-655-9

Cover design: JulesRulesDesign
Text design: Lisa Taylor
Photographs: Gregory E. Lang

Printed in Canada
2 3 4 5 6 7 8 — 12 11 10 09 08 07

On behalf of my brothers, David, Kevin, and Jody,
and myself, this book is lovingly dedicated to
Gloria Dianne Brown Lang, our mom.

INTRODUCTION

On my mantelpiece rests an aging photograph of my mother that was taken as she was about to graduate from high school, a few short years before she chose to alter her life and become a mother. She was beautiful then, with hair that fell upon her shoulders, big eyes that reassured, and a smile that warmed. I am told she was energetic, vivacious, and popular back then, when she was young and had only herself to be concerned about. This photograph is my favorite picture of my mother, and although it has yellowed and faded, it has been lovingly displayed wherever I have lived and serves to remind me of the nest from which I flew, the home my mother kept for my four siblings and me, and the bosom to which I always return—one of unconditional love and acceptance.

My memories of childhood include the many things my mother did to make sure my siblings and I were well cared for and happy. Every day began with a hot breakfast, often including biscuits made from scratch, lunchboxes were filled with what we each liked to eat, and dinner always included someone's favorite food. With a family so large, cooking consumed much of her time. My passion for cooking and belief that it is a sincere gesture of love can be traced back to my mother and the way she never failed to bake a birthday cake of choice, bring soup to the child sick in bed, alter recipes to suit our tastes, and make the house *smell* like the approaching season or holiday. But my mother did far more than cook for us to let us know she loved us.

She made clothes for us, tended to our scrapes and cuts, drove us to our respective after-school activities and cheered us on, sought out obscure but coveted gifts for Christmas, helped with difficult homework assignments, wiped tears away and endured tantrums, all the while making sure not a child was overlooked, doing or giving whatever each needed, as though she had nothing more important to do. My mother helped me negotiate my conflicts with my dad, taught me to ride a bicycle, balance a checkbook, sew on a button, check a turkey for doneness, change a diaper, treat a cold, and, years later, how to determine what my own infant needed when she cried. My mother did many other things for me that taken one at a time may seem inconsequential, but when taken all together, made me who I am. She also did things for me that others are unaware of, and knowing her, I am confident I am not alone in that privilege. But still, my mother did far more than these kinds of everyday maternal tasks to let us know she loved us.

Each son eventually presented our parents with a unique set of challenges, and my mother was unfailing in her ability to deal with what came. If she was ever disappointed in us, any sign of it was overshadowed by her actions. One son got into trouble, and my mother was there to help find a different path. One fell on hard times, and my mother was there to help ease the burden until times got better. Another could not see beyond a broken heart, and my mother was there to offer comfort and bring hope. One child became sick, and my mother was there to provide care. Our mother has loved us collectively, but also individually in a way that expresses to each of us, in the way that only a mother can express, that she is, and shall remain, there for us, no matter what. Gone from her nest but never from her heart, fully grown but always her beloved son or little girl, each can call upon her still, and she will come. It is this, her unwavering devotion, her tireless effort to help, her unshakable faith in our goodness, her absolute belief in our worth, that let us know then and lets us know now, that we are loved.

I am the first of five children, and over the forty-plus years since my birth I have seen much about my mother change, and I have seen much remain the same. Although now much older than the young woman pictured in the photograph I treasure, her eyes still offer reassurance to whomever she gazes upon, as does the gentle touch she gives while listening intently to whatever one shares with her. Her smile still warms, as does her laughter and the heartfelt embrace all have come to expect when coming upon her. I still receive birthday cards, enjoy a favorite meal when I go home, and hear from her the applause and affirmations that tell me she is proud of my accomplishments. Now walking more slowly, her hands less able than they once were, her health requiring more and more concessions from her, she struggles at times to keep up her former pace. Yet, in spite of these changes, she always manages to *be there* when needed.

I do not know what my mother's dreams were, what plans she had in mind for herself as she grew up, where she wanted to visit or what she might have become if she had chosen to live her life differently. I am ashamed that I do not know these things because I have never thought to ask, but I also do not know because my mother has never uttered a word of disappointment about the life she has lived. I do not know of her regrets for she does not share them, if they exist, nor does she lament about what her life used to be like or otherwise give off signs of disappointment about what age has taken from her. Perhaps she has just accepted her life for what it is, thinking it is too late to change it. Or, perhaps she is happy with her life for what it has been. It is the latter, I like to think, because I know my mother has enjoyed being a mother, and a grandmother, and a surrogate mother or grandmother to those in need who have been fortunate enough to enter her life. I know this because she never fails to seize the opportunity to act like a mom, to be there for someone.

I love my mother dearly, and I have a long list of things I want to do for her one day, but most of all I want to tell her "thank you." I believe that a child, especially a son, can never express enough gratitude for what a mother has done. I know that I cannot, but I know what I will do to try. I will do what my mother did for me. I will be there when she needs me, no matter what. I love you, Mom.

WHY A SON NEEDS A MOM

A son needs a mom

to tell him he is handsome.

A son needs a mom

to see that he does not become spoiled.

A son needs a mom . . .

to teach him that embarrassment is not
a reason for quitting.

to teach him to play fair.

to believe in him even when it seems no one else does.

A son needs a mom . . .

to assure him that his heartache will not last forever.

to help him see the richness of diversity.

to teach him to show appreciation for what
others have done for him.

A son needs a mom

to be his trusted confidante.

A son needs a mom . . .

to help him understand that things will not always go his way.

to teach him to pay attention to the small things.

to teach him that every fight isn't worth fighting.

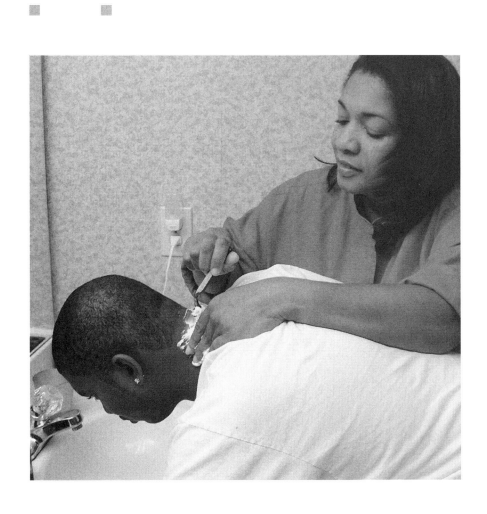

A son needs a mom

to make sure he looks his best
before leaving the house.

A son needs a mom . . .

to make sure that faith is the light that guides him.

to tell him that anything is possible if done
for the right reason.

to tell him that remaining faithful is his
promise and obligation.

A son needs a mom

to steer him away from darkness.

A son needs a mom . . .

who sees the humor in his silly ways.

who insists that he do his fair share of the
household chores.

who will stand up to him when he is wrong.

who encourages self-expression.

A son needs a mom

to protect him until he is old enough
to protect himself.

A son needs a mom . . .

to make sure he attends to his mind, as well as his body.

to teach him that admitting one's mistakes is a
sign of strength, not weakness.

to tell him that he cannot change others, but he can
learn to accept them for who they are.

A son needs a mom

to teach him that all people are worthy of respect.

A son needs a mom

to help him overcome his fears.

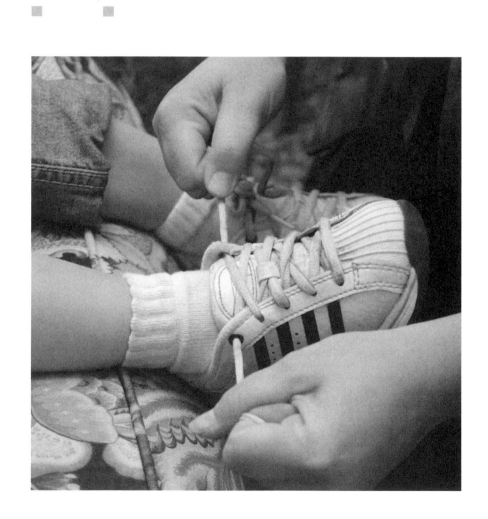

A son needs a mom

to make sure his socks match.

A son needs a mom

who doesn't forget that boys will be boys.

A son needs a mom . . .

who will not fail to discipline him for his misdeeds.

to tell him often that he is loved.

to help him understand and respect personal space.

A son needs a mom . . .

to make his favorite food on his birthday.

to help him learn how to laugh at himself.

to help him develop the habits girls prize.

to teach him that being subtle can be attractive.

A son needs a mom

to hold him when he needs comfort.

A son needs a mom

who understands the pleasure of a good pillow fight.

A son needs a mom

who will let him be himself.

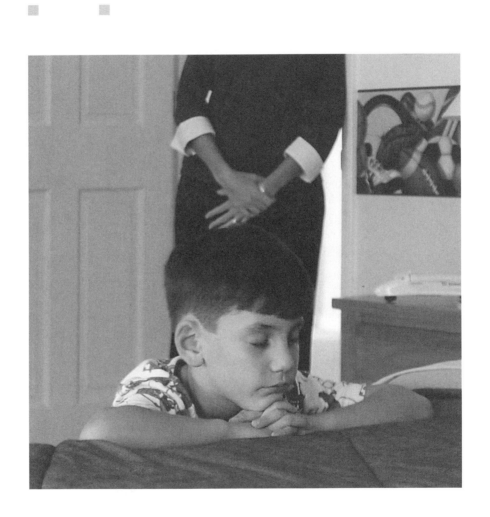

A son needs a mom

to remind him to say his prayers.

A son needs a mom . . .

to teach him that he can be competitive
without being ruthless.

to teach him to avoid selfish temptations.

to teach him to try harder when given a second chance.

to teach him that family is more important than work.

A son needs a mom

to make sure his world has a broad horizon.

A son needs a mom

to make sure he has good memories to hold on to.

■   ■   ■   ■   ■   ■   ■

A son needs a mom

to make sure he begins his day on the right foot.

A son needs a mom . . .

who knows where to find what he has misplaced.

who understands that what he needs from her
changes as he grows older.

who leads him toward his talents and passions.

who is never more than a phone call away.

A son needs a mom

to teach him how to take care of himself.

A son needs a mom

who does not hold him back when he is
ready to take the next step.

A son needs a mom

who is there for him no matter what his age.

A son needs a mom

to teach him how to flirt without making a fool of himself.

A son needs a mom . . .

to let him know it is okay to cry.

to be his first dance partner.

to show him what it means to love unconditionally.

to help him understand the secrets of girls.

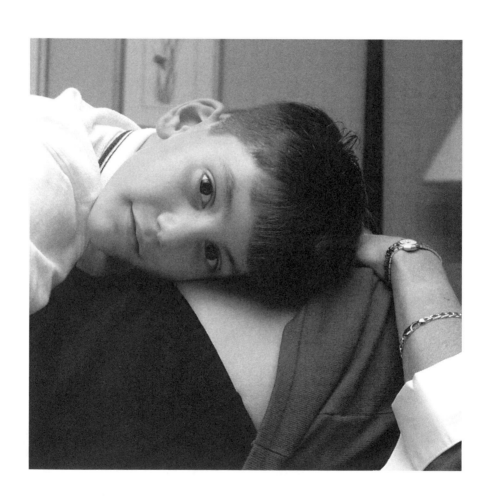

A son needs a mom

to tell him about the miracle of life.

A son needs a mom

to show him how to take one day at a time.

A son needs a mom

who laughs at his jokes.

A son needs a mom

who will indulge his love of action.

A son needs a mom

who allows him to be her protector now and then.

A son needs a mom

who will make sure he does not get
lost in the crowd.

A son needs a mom . . .

to teach him the pitfalls of hypocrisy.

to be his strength when he is weak.

to teach him that sometimes the battle is within.

A son needs a mom

who understands that boys like big toys.

A son needs a mom

to tell him that jealousy can ruin a relationship.

A son needs a mom . . .

to help him attend to the details girls will notice.

who will let him go when he is ready to marry.

to help prepare him for being a father.

A son needs a mom . . .

whose arms, heart, and mind are always open.

who knows how to have fun.

who never tires of his hugs and kisses.

A son needs a mom

to teach him the art of listening.

A son needs a mom

to make sure he finishes his homework first.

A son needs a mom . . .

to advise him when he falls in love.

to teach him to be a force of kindness in the world.

to explain to him what he cannot yet understand.

to tell him that there is more to being a man
than being tough.

A son needs a mom

who is always excited to hear his news.

A son needs a mom

to teach him that a sense of humor
will never lose its luster.

A son needs a mom . . .

who is always there for him, even if by mail.

to insist that he be respectful of women.

to tell him that women admire a sincere apology.

A son needs a mom

to make sure there is no room
for bitterness in his heart.

A son needs a mom

to fill his childhood with love and affection.

A son needs a mom

who will always make sure he has
a home to come back to.

A son needs a mom

who shows him that men and women are equals.

A son needs a mom . . .

to teach him table manners.

to teach him that he should be humble.

to help him develop sound financial habits.

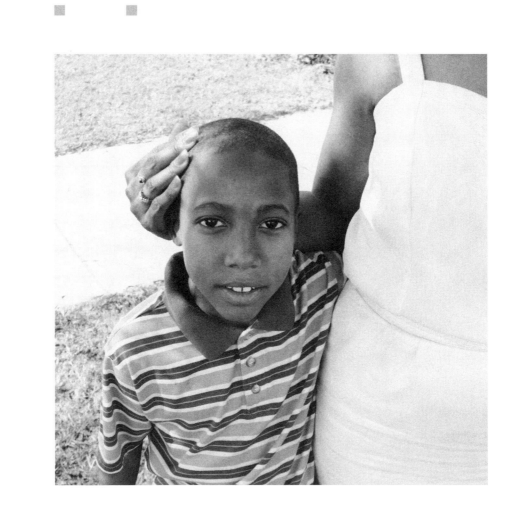

A son needs a mom

to teach him how to conduct himself
like a gentleman.

■　　　■　　　■　　　■　　　■　　　■　　　■

A son needs a mom

to teach him how to show love without restraint.

A son needs a mom . . .

to encourage him to be serious about his work.

to make sacrifices so he will not have to sacrifice.

to teach him the importance of compromise.

A son needs a mom

because without her he will have less
in his life than he deserves.

ACKNOWLEDGMENTS

This book could not have been written without the support and generosity of many people. I offer a special thanks to the sons and moms who posed for me, who invited me into their lives and homes, who cooperated with my schedule and sometimes strange requests, and who helped me to better put into words and pictures why sons need their moms.

I also wish to thank the administration of Greater Atlanta Christian School, which helped me once more to recruit families to participate in creating this book, Becky Lang who also helped recruit families, and Diane Hileman of Mothers & More, who, although we have never met, extended a great helping hand in finding sons and moms.

Finally, I wish to thank Ron Pitkin and the staff at Cumberland House, including my editor, Lisa Taylor, who once again pushed me to make sure this book became what it could be. I also want to give a special thanks to Julie Jayne, whose faith in each book has been a key contributor to the success of the series. Julie, you have my deepest appreciation and warmest regards.

TO CONTACT THE AUTHOR

write in care of the publisher:

Cumberland House Publishing
431 Harding Industrial Drive
Nashville, TN 37211

email the author or visit his Web site:

greg.lang@mindspring.com
www. gregoryelang.com